D0907183

Creative Crafts
for kids

Scrapbook Starters

Tracy Nelson Maurer

ROURKE PUBLISHING

Vero Beach, Florida 32964

www.rourkepublishing.com

Please do not leave sharp or small objects or permanent pens where very young hands can find them.

Author Acknowledgments
Thank you to Meg, Tommy, Kim and the crews at Rourke and Blue Door. Thank you to Ashley Wierback for producing the projects for photography.

Photo credits: All photos by Blue Door Publishing except Cover © Jaimie Duplass; Title Page © Jaimie Duplass; Contents Page © Pinkcandy; Page 4 © marymary, argus, Albert Campbell, Rob Marmion, sonya etchison, Alina Solovyova-Vincent; Page 5 © Katrina Brown, Jaimie Duplass, Darren Baker, Monkey Business Images; Page 6 © Valerie Loiseleux, Elena Schweitzer, Shmeliova Natalia, willy12; Page 7 © Shmeliova Natalia, Cecilia Bajic; Page 8 © Eric Cote; Page 9 © Sonya Etchison, Rob Marmion, Alina Solovyova-Vincent; Page 11 © Katrina Brown, Nicolette Neish; Page 12 © Blue Door Publishing; Page 13 © Blue Door Publishing; Page 14 © vectorstock; Page 15 © XPhantom, Rob Marmion, vectorstock, Maria Bell; Page 16 © chispas, Blue Door Publishing, Paul B. Moore, Jason Stitt, Denise Kappa; Page 17 © chispas, Blue Door Publishing; Page 18 © Blue Door Publishing, Mark Breck, Vibrant Image Studio, Varina and Jay Patel, Studio 1One; Page 19 © Blue Door Publishing, Mark Breck, Vibrant Image Studio, Varina and Jay Patel, Studio 1One; Page 20 © Kaycee Craig, Yei; Page 21 © Sonya Etchison, Noam Armonn, Blue Door Publishing, Yei; Page 22 © Blue Door Publishing; Page 23 © Blue Door Publishing; Page 25 © Katrina Brown, Vadim Volodin, Monkey Business Images, chispas; Page 26 © Blue Door Publishing; Page 27 © Blue Door Publishing; Page 28 © Blue Door Publishing, Allison; Page 29 © Blue Door Publishing, Allison, Katrina Brown; Page 30 © Alina Solovyova-Vincent, Monkey Business Images, chispas; Page 31 © chispas; Page 32 © chispas

Editor: Meg Greve

Cover and page design by Nicola Stratford, Blue Door Publishing

Library of Congress Cataloging-in-Publication Data

  Maurer, Tracy, 1965-
Scrapbook starters / Tracy Nelson Maurer.
    p. cm. -- (Creative crafts for kids)
  Includes index.
  ISBN 978-1-60694-343-4 (hard cover)
  ISBN 978-1-60694-505-6 (soft cover)
  1. Photograph albums--Juvenile literature. 2. Photographs--Conservation and restoration--Juvenile literature. 3. Scrapbooks--Juvenile literature. I. Title.
  TR465.M395 2009
  745.593--dc22
                        2009003900
Printed in the USA

www.rourkepublishing.com - rourke@rourkepublishing.com
Post Office Box 643328 Vero Beach, Florida 32964

Contents

tell Your story

What exciting experiences, important events, or special people make you smile when you think of them? Making a scrapbook, also known as scrapbooking, is a way to tell a story about yourself with pictures and notes.

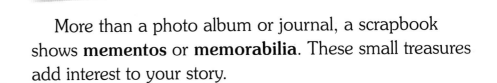

More than a photo album or journal, a scrapbook shows **mementos** or **memorabilia**. These small treasures add interest to your story.

What's Your Theme?

A theme describes your scrapbook story. It ties the pictures, words, and mementos together. Choose photographs and mementos that best **illustrate** your theme.

Give your scrapbook project a title. The title usually describes the theme, such as *Pizza Is My Favorite Food* or simply, *Mmmmm!*

Save wrapping paper from your presents to create a birthday scrapbook.

think theme

Jump-start your scrapbook projects with these theme ideas.

- beach fun
- birthday party
- books or movies
- camping or fishing
- family gathering
- favorite food
- favorite sport
- field trip
- first day of school
- first pet
- holidays
- moving day
- music or bands
- school club
- sleepover
- vacations
- your room

Gather Materials

Gathering materials is the scrapbooker's treasure hunt. Look for mementos that focus on your theme, such as a program from a play or a ticket from a game. Flat mementos work best for most projects.

TiP

Store paper mementos in clear sheet protectors to avoid creases. Put your other treasures in clear zipper bags.

Collect pretty papers to use for your backgrounds.

T i P

For pressed flowers, pick small blossoms. Place them on a page in a heavy phone book and close book. The flat flowers are ready to use in about a week.

Memento Ideas

Need more ideas for your collection? Try any of these.

- buttons and pins
- magazine clippings
- ribbons or bows
- printouts of clip art
- awards, certificates
- copies of letters
- fabric scraps
- handprints
- menus or coasters
- postcards, greeting cards, recipe cards
- seed envelopes, seeds,
- pressed flowers and leaves
- small pebbles, shells
- stickers, postage stamps

Starter Supplies

- colored construction paper and white typing paper
- sharp scissors
- clear ruler
- masking tape
- clear drying tacky glue and glue sticks
- variety of markers, both permanent and washable
- gel pens

Craft stores sell all kinds of fancy supplies. Wait to stock up on expensive specialty decorations and **archival** materials until after you practice on a few projects.

Basic Rules for Scrapbooking

1. Ask an adult to help you, especially if you are working with glass or sharp tools.
2. Get permission before you cut a photograph or glue a keepsake. Use only **duplicates** or copies of photos.
3. Cover your work area with plastic or an old tablecloth. Clean up when you are done.

T i P

Use a photo labeling pencil, also called a grease pencil, to write on the picture. Note names, date, place, and fun facts. You can wipe away the grease later with a soft tissue. Most craft stores sell grease pencils.

Ask family and friends for duplicate pictures. Digital photos can also be printed from your home computer.

organizing supplies

- clear medium or large zipper bags
- clear sheet protectors that open at the top
- permanent marker to label the bags and sheet protectors
- shoeboxes
- notebook or journal

organize your stuff

Hunting for treasured mementos is fun. Searching for lost scissors is not. Organize your materials before and after you work on a project.

Sort photos and mementos by subject or date. Use a shoebox or plastic bin to hold your scrapbooking supplies.

TIP

Plan ahead. Write ideas for future scrapbooks in a notebook with a list of supplies. When you shop, bring your notebook.

Many craft stores sell scrapbook kits that include materials for creating theme pages.

Mermaid Bay

Plastic bins with small compartments keep your tiny treasures organized.

- shoebox with lid
- covering material
- 2 pieces of felt
- tacky glue
- scissors
- fabric scissors
- large index cards
- permanent marker
- scrapbook mementos, ribbons, or other decorations

T i P

For covering materials, try wrapping paper, 1/2 yard (.5 meter) of cotton fabric, foil, shelf liner, Sunday comics, paper grocery bags, used gift bags, or paint.

organizer Scrapbook Box

Turn your shoebox organizer into a useful scrapbook. Give your box a theme and title, such as *Supplies* or *School Days*. Match your covering material to your theme. Decorate the box with photos and mementos. Write notes on the box about your projects.

Here's How:

1. Cut the covering to fit around the outside and inside of box. Do the same for the lid. Wrap each one as if you are wrapping a gift. Glue the covering to the box and to the lid.

2. Trace the lid onto each piece of felt. Cut about 1/4 inch (.6 cm) inside the tracing lines, so the felt is smaller than the lid.

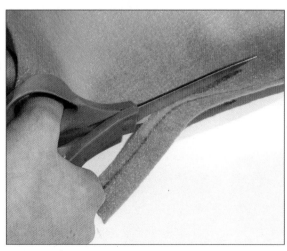

3. Glue one felt sheet inside the lid and one inside on the bottom of the box.

4. Label the box with the marker and decorate with mementos.

5. As you add supplies, photos, or mementos in your box, use the index cards to keep the items sorted. Label the index cards.

13

You Will Need:

- one piece of construction paper
- three pictures of you cooking, baking, or eating your favorite foods
- two flat mementos, such as recipe cards, package labels, or party napkins
- pencil
- masking tape
- tacky glue
- scissors
- markers

Favorite Foods Scrapbook Page

A scrapbook page needs a **layout**, or a design, to show off your pictures and mementos. Use an odd number of photos, usually three or five. Try different layouts with the *Favorite Foods* scrapbook page.

Here's How:

1. Arrange the pictures and mementos in a layout that you like.

2. Keep some empty areas, called **negative space**, to focus attention on your pictures. Negative space also gives you room to write notes, an important part of scrapbooking.

3. Mark with a light pencil line where you want to place your items.

4. Lift one item at a time to glue it, leaving the others in place. Let it dry.

5. Write *Mmmm* in big letters on the page with the markers. Add a happy memory about each of your favorite foods. Write the date.

Try placing items in a different order, overlapping two, or connecting them with string, arrows, or other designs.

Mmmmm!

My favorite f

Mmmmm!
COOKIES are my favorite!

Baking with my mom

December 09

You Will Need:

- one 8 x 10 inch (20 x 25 centimeter) wooden frame
- one piece of orange construction paper
- three Halloween cookie cutters
- three pictures from Halloween
- two flat mementos (Halloween stickers, candy bar wrappers, fake spider webs)
- pencil
- masking tape
- glow-in-the-dark paint
- tacky glue
- scissors
- markers

Halloween Scrapbook Frame

Day or night, this scrapbook scares up your fun Halloween memories. Glow-in-the-dark paint or stickers add to the fun.

Here's How:

1. Ask an adult to remove the frame's glass. Use the pencil to trace inside the frame's opening onto the construction paper. Cut about 1/4 inch (.6 centimeter) outside the lines, so the paper will be slightly larger than the opening.

2. Trace inside the cookie cutters onto the paper and cut out the shapes. Leave space for a title and notes.

3. Tape a photo behind each hole. Trim any overlapping photos. Glue mementos onto the paper. Outline each of the shapes and mementos with markers or glow-in-the-dark paint.

4. Let it dry for 24 hours before you ask an adult to reassemble the frame.

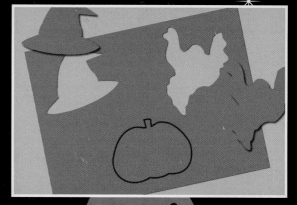

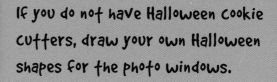

TIP

If you do not have Halloween cookie cutters, draw your own Halloween shapes for the photo windows.

You Will Need:

- clear ball-shaped plastic or glass ornament with removable hanger
- three small photos from a day at the beach
- light blue construction paper
- a quarter
- small mementos (3 small scoops of clean sand, pebbles, shells, rhinestones)
- grease pencil
- pencil
- fabric paint
- glue stick
- paper scissors
- markers

Memory Ball Scrapbook

You can see this scrapbook from every side. Hang the memory ball from a curtain rod or decorate an egg carton section to hold it.

Here's How:

1. Place the coin over a face in a picture. Trace around the quarter with the grease pencil, and cut out the circle. Wipe off extra grease. Glue one picture onto the construction paper. Cut around the photo, leaving about 1/4 inch (.6 cm) to make a round frame. Repeat with your other pictures.

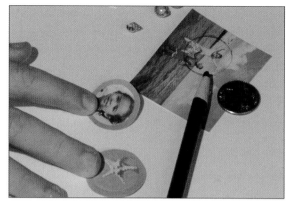

2. On the back of the photo discs, write words or phrases that remind you of that day.

3. Use the fabric paint to write the title of your memory ball on the glass. Let it dry.

4. After an adult removes the hanger, add sand and mementos to the ornament. Watch for sharp edges!

5. Slightly curl the photo discs and push through the top. Replace the top.

- folder with clasps and pockets
- three sheets of construction paper
- hole punch
- pencil
- markers
- glue stick
- photos and mementos

Paper punchers in fun shapes can be found at most craft stores. Use the punched out shapes to decorate your pages as well.

Friends Forever Folder

Make a scrapbook about your friends. This project starts with three friends and has room for many more. Add pages when you meet new friends.

Here's How:

1. Decorate the folder, adding mementos and photos inside and on the cover. Write the title on the cover, or use sticky letters.

2. Decorate each sheet of construction paper for a different friend. Show where you met, favorite things about your friend, and things you have done together. Leave about 2 inches (5 centimeters) on the left side of the page for the clasps.

3. Mark where the clasps line up on the paper. Punch holes in the paper and assemble the scrapbook.

Choose construction paper in your friends' favorite colors.

CHELSEA

FRIENDS FOREVER

SOPHIA

- 15 inches (38 centimeters) of ribbon
- five sheets of construction paper
- one sheet of felt
- scissors
- glue stick
- tacky glue
- markers
- photos and mementos

Make your foldout scrapbook longer by folding and gluing more pages.

Family Foldout Scrapbook

Gather your family photographs, mementos, and special memories in one scrapbook that folds out like an **accordion**. Give it to a grandparent as a brag book. An older brother or sister serving in the armed forces far away would treasure this scrapbook, too.

Here's How:

1. Fold two sheets of construction paper in half. Stand them side by side with their folded edges facing out (a).

   Fold a third sheet of paper and glue the inside right half of this to the inside right of the first paper (b).

   Fold a fourth sheet of paper and glue the inside of this to the next part of the zig-zag (c).

   Continue gluing the zigzag with the fifth sheet of paper (d).

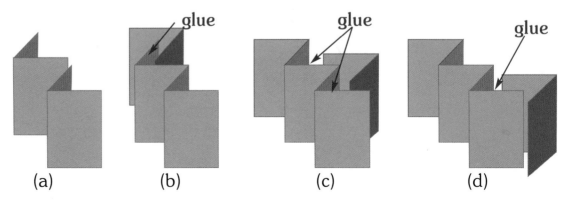

(a)　　　　(b)　　　　(c)　　　　(d)

2. Fold the scrapbook together. Glue the ribbon across the back. Cut the felt so that it is the same size as the back. Spread tacky glue over the back. Glue the felt onto the back over the ribbon.

3. Title your scrapbook and decorate the cover and inside pages with pictures and mementos. Write a letter or a poem about your family on the back.

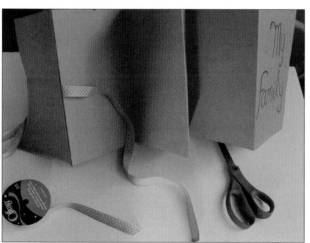

T i P

For a soldier, use a yellow ribbon. It is a symbol of hope for a safe return.

23

- one calendar or date book
- 12 sheets of construction paper
- cookie cutters
- coffee mug
- quarter
- scissors
- pencil
- grease pencil
- glue stick
- markers
- photos and mementos

calendar scrapbook

Sometimes stores and banks give customers small date books. You can also find calendars to print out on the Internet. Ask an adult to help you. Why look at a plain year, when you can decorate a calendar your way?

Here's How:

1. Cut the construction paper and glue it to cover the calendar pages without dates.

2. Give each month a theme and title. Match cookie cutters to the theme. The coffee mug and the quarter are **templates**, too. Using the grease pencil, trace the templates onto the photos or colored paper. Cut out the shapes.

3. Glue pictures and mementos on each month. Leave space for a title and notes.

July						
SUNDAY	MONDAY	TUESDAY	WEDNESDAY	THURSDAY	FRIDAY	SATURDAY
31	1	2	3	4 Independence Day :)	5	6
7	8	9	10	11	12	13

BACK **2** School

My Class

My Friends

ⓣ ⓘ ⓟ

If you have small photos of family and friends, glue their pictures on their birthdays.

September

SUNDAY	MONDAY	TUESDAY	WEDNESDAY	THURSDAY	FRI
31	1	2	3	4	5	6
7	8 First Day of School!	9	10	11	12	13
14	15	16	17	18	19	

You Will Need:

- one old hardcover book
- shopping bag paper
- construction paper in
  1 x 3 inch (2.5 x 8
  centimeter)
  rectangles
- scissors
- pencil
- glue stick
- markers
- photos and mementos

All About Me Scrapbook

Turn old books from yard sales into instant scrapbooks. To start, write about yourself in a notebook. Make lists of your favorite things, best friends, hobbies, and memorable moments.

Use your notes to decide how to organize the book. Maybe each chapter will show a different year, your favorite team, or a hobby.

26

Here's How:

1. Glue the new paper cover onto the old cover. Write your title on the cover and decorate it.

2. Make tabs. Write a chapter title on each rectangle. Glue the lower half of each tab to the side of its chapter page.

3. Glue pictures, mementos, poems, or your lists. Be sure to write the dates on the pages.

If the old book has a lot of pages, fill it over time instead of all at once.

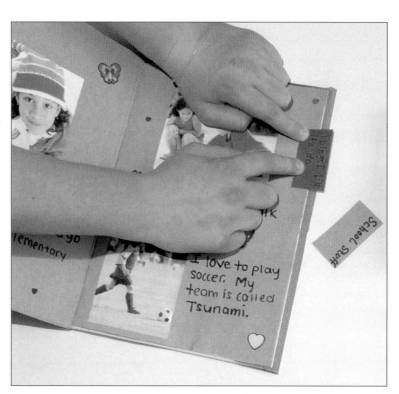

- fabric or other sturdy material
- tacky glue
- scissors
- pencil
- small buttons, glitter, smaller pieces of fabric, or ribbon

Tip

Use glue sticks for paper, such as photographs. Use tacky glue for heavier items, such as fabric.

Scrap Pocket

Keep your extra pictures and mementos in a scrap pocket for almost any scrapbook. Use construction paper, wallpaper, fabric, felt, wax paper, or any other strong material.

Here's How:

1. Choose a shape, such as a heart, fish, or tree. Your shape can match your theme, such as an apple for school, or a flip-flop for summer vacations. Draw it on the pocket material smaller than the scrapbook page. Cut out the shape.

2. Decorate the shape.

3. Put glue on the shape's back edges, making a strip of glue along the two sides and bottom. Do not put glue on the top edge. Place the shape on the scrapbook page. Let it dry before you put anything in your pocket.

For an easy and fast pocket, glue the front side of an envelope onto the page of your scrapbook.

29

Keep Scrapping!

This book offers some ideas to start your scrapbooks. Try different colors, sizes, or materials. Experiment with designs that are more complex. Craft stores and websites offer kits, supplies, and more scrapbook ideas. Do your friends have scrapbooks? Start a scrapbooking club and share the fun!

T i P

After each scrapbook project, write in your notebook what worked well and what you want to try next time.

Glossary

accordion (uh-KOR-dee-uhn): a musical instrument that you squeeze to make sound

archival (ar-KYV-ul): known not to damage material over many years

duplicates (DOO-pli-kits): copies of original work

illustrate (IL-uh-strate): to show or explain using pictures

layout (LAY-out): the placement of images on a page or work of art

mementos (me-MEN-toz): things that recall a person, place, or other part of the past

memorabilia (MEM-ur-uh-beel-ya): things that recall a person, place, or other part of the past

negative space (NEG-uh-tiv SPAYS): the unused part of a page or work of art

templates (TEM-playts): tools used as guides for tracing

Index

Websites to Visit

http://familyfun.go.com/parties/birthday/feature/kids-crafting-party/kids-crafting-party.html

home.howstuffworks.com/scrapbook-crafts.htm

www.makingfriends.com/scrapbook_kids.htm

www.scrapbook.com/

www.scrapbook-art.net/scrapbooking-advice.html

www.thatscrapbooksite.com/

About the Author

Tracy Nelson Maurer has written more than 60 fiction and nonfiction books for children. She loved crafts as a child and she still likes to take the scissors for a whirl. Tracy lives near Minneapolis, Minnesota, with her husband and two children.